Samuel French Acting Edition

C000103710

A Candle on the Table

by Patricia Clapp

SAMUELFRENCH.COM SAMUELFRENCH.CO.UK

FOR PRODUCTION ENQUIRIES

UNITED STATES AND CANADA
Info@SamuelFrench.com
1-866-598-8449

UNITED KINGDOM AND EUROPE
Plays@SamuelFrench.co.uk
020-7255-4302

Each title is subject to availability from Samuel French, depending upon country of performance. Please be aware that A CANDLE ON THE TABLE may not be licensed by Samuel French in your territory. Professional and amateur producers should contact the nearest Samuel French office or licensing partner to verify availability.

Please refer to page 22 for further copyright information.

STORY OF THE PLAY

Three elderly women meet at a lunch table on their first day in a home for senior citizens. A candle placed there by their matron, Mrs. Hodges, awakens different memories in each. To the frivolous, friendly ex-actress, Maribeth Garrity, candles belong with champagne and flowers. To Miss Tolliver, a children's nursemaid, they speak of childhood poverty when candles gave the only light. To the aristocratic Mrs. Bramson they mean the formal dinner parties which only emphasized the emptiness of her life. The lunchtime conversation reveals some surprising aspects of the lives and personalities of the three women, and culminates in a friendship and an affirmative decision.

3

CHARACTERS

Mrs. Bramson, *an aristocrat.*
Mrs. Hodges, *matron of the home.*
Miss Tolliver, *an ex-nursemaid.*
Mrs. Garrity, *an ex-actress.*

Scene: Dining room of a home for senior citizens.

Time: The present.

A Candle on the Table

SCENE: *There is a small table, covered with a cloth, and set for three. Three chairs are drawn up to it. Near it is a small table or buffet on which a tray can be set.*

(As the Curtain Rises *we see* Mrs. Bramson *sitting at the table. She is an elderly woman, very much the wealthy dowager. She wears an attractive dress, with tasteful touches of jewelry, and has a small purse. In spite of her apparent poise we sense a touch of nervousness as she straightens the silver slightly or turns her water glass in her fingers. Almost immediately* Mrs. Hodges *enters, followed by* Miss Tolliver. Mrs. Hodges *is in her 50's, neatly dressed. She is a busy woman, with a rather professional smile, but there is a great deal of warmth underneath.* Miss Tolliver *is elderly. Her clothes are neat and clean and somehow manage to look like a uniform. Her hair is tidily, but not becomingly arranged, and she is both shy and ill at ease.* Mrs. Bramson *looks up as the two women approach the table.*)

Mrs. Hodges. Mrs. Bramson? (*She receives a formal nod.*) This is Miss Tolliver. Since this is the first day here for both of you I thought I would seat you at the same table so you can get acquainted. (*She smiles and pulls out a chair for* Miss Tolliver.)

Mrs. Bramson (*stiffly*). How do you do.

Miss Tolliver (*sliding into the chair*). How do you do, Mrs. Bramson.

Mrs. Hodges. There will be one more lady here—Mrs. Garrity. I've put you three newcomers all together for today, but of course we can always change later on.

Mrs. Bramson (*glancing at her watch*). This—Mrs. Garrity has not arrived yet?

Mrs. Hodges. Oh, yes, she's here. I expect she'll be along in a moment or two.

5

Mrs. Bramson. I understood that luncheon was at half past twelve. It is now—

Mrs. Hodges (*interrupting, but pleasantly*). Oh, we're not quite that rigid, Mrs. Bramson. Almost any time between twelve and one o'clock is all right.

Mrs. Bramson. I do not enjoy waiting for my meals.

Mrs. Hodges (*soothingly*). I'm sure Mrs. Garrity will be right along. You two just get acquainted while you're waiting. (*With a last smile* Mrs. Hodges *exits.*)

Mrs. Bramson. So discourteous, I always think, to be late for meals.

Miss Tolliver (*hesitantly*). Perhaps she didn't know. What time lunch was, I mean.

Mrs. Bramson. It was stated quite clearly on a large card posted in my room. I assume there was a similar card in her room, as well as yours, Mrs.—Tolliver?

Miss Tolliver. *Miss. Miss* Tolliver.

Mrs. Bramson. Oh, yes. I am Mrs. Bramson, Miss Tolliver. Mrs. Wadsworth Bramson the Third.

Miss Tolliver. Yes. Mrs. Hodges told me. I am glad to know you, Mrs. Bramson.

Mrs. Bramson. I believe Mrs. Hodges said you had just arrived here, Miss Tolliver?

Miss Tolliver. That's right. Just an hour or so ago. (*Hesitantly.*) It seems quite a nice place, I think, don't you?

Mrs. Bramson. It is not unattractive, but I am not at all sure about the service. Half past twelve, the card said quite plainly. Luncheon is served at half past twelve.

Miss Tolliver. It can't be much past that now. I noticed the clock in the main room as I came through—it said twenty-five minutes of one.

Mrs. Bramson (*firmly*). Twenty-five minutes of one is *not* half past twelve!

Miss Tolliver (*defeated*). No, I suppose it's not.

(*There is a small pause.*)

Mrs. Bramson. Garrity. Rather a common name, isn't it? But then, I suppose at a place like this we shall meet all sorts of people.

Miss Tolliver. I suppose so. I rather hope so.

MRS. BRAMSON. Well, we need not be friends with them unless we choose. Mr. Bramson always preferred to have many *acquaintances*, but few friends. He felt there were not many people he really wanted to have as close friends.

MISS TOLLIVER. Oh?

MRS. BRAMSON. Oh, there were plenty who would have *liked* to be close to him. Don't misunderstand me. Whenever he chose to entertain—when *we* chose, I mean—no one ever refused an invitation. Never.

MISS TOLLIVER (*making conversation*). Did you have many parties?

MRS. BRAMSON. I should hardly call them "parties." Dinners, generally. Mr. Bramson liked to entertain formally. Usually it was for business reasons, you know. He would signal me when to leave the table with the other women, and then the men would discuss business affairs. Very influential men, they were.

MISS TOLLIVER. I'm sure. It must have been very pleasant for you—entertaining so beautifully.

MRS. BRAMSON. Pleasant? I never really thought of it as being a pleasure. It was a great responsibility. When Mr. Bramson was pleased I was very satisfied, of course. He was very particular about how everything was done. (*A glance at her watch.*) He would *never* have stood for a guest being late for a meal! Never!

MISS TOLLIVER. But Mrs. Garrity is not exactly our guest, is she? (*A silence.* MISS TOLLIVER *tries another shy gambit.*) Mrs. Hodges seems a pleasant woman.

MRS. BRAMSON. That is, after all, her job. As hostess, or matron, or whatever she chooses to call herself, she *should* be pleasant.

MISS TOLLIVER. But it can't always be easy.

MRS. BRAMSON. It's what she is paid to do. *Highly* paid, too, no doubt. Wages, these days, are unthinkable!

MISS TOLLIVER. I am sure she works hard.

MRS. BRAMSON. Hard work never hurt anyone yet. She is fortunate to have such a responsible position. Quite like a housekeeper, I imagine.

MISS TOLLIVER (*quickly*). Oh, more than that, I think.

MRS. BRAMSON. A competent housekeeper is very valuable. I have had several over the years—honest, hardworking women who earned their salaries with no nonsense.

MISS TOLLIVER. You were very lucky to find them.

MRS. BRAMSON. I trained them, Miss Tolliver. I trained them! They started out as housemaids and worked up over the years. Mr. Bramson always said that was the only way to get good servants. Haven't you found it so?

MISS TOLLIVER (*with a tiny smile*). In a way, perhaps, I have.

MRS. BRAMSON. Although, since you are *Miss* Tolliver, perhaps you did not have your own establishment?

MISS TOLLIVER. No, I didn't really. But I still know quite a bit about—good servants.

(MRS. HODGES *appears with* MRS. GARRITY. *She is a gay, warm, pretty, elderly woman, rather given to ruffles and ribbons and curls. There is a very girlish quality about her which is delightful.*)

MRS. HODGES. Here she is—Mrs. Garrity, this is Mrs. Bramson and Miss Tolliver. I am sure you are going to like each other. (*She holds a chair for* MRS. GARRITY *who settles herself happily into it.*)

MRS. GARRITY. Oh, I do hope I haven't kept you waiting! I did want to unpack and put my things around—I think a room always looks more homelike with all one's own things around, don't you? It's always the first thing I do—but it took longer than I thought. I can never put a photograph album away without looking through it first—so silly of me—

MRS. HODGES. I'll bring your lunch right along now. It's rather a busy day for us on Saturdays—a lot of guests, you know—so I'm giving the waitresses a hand. It will just be a moment or two.

MRS. GARRITY (*lightly*). Don't hurry, love. We're not going anywhere. (*Laughs.* MRS. HODGES *smiles and exits. Spreading her napkin on her lap.*) Mrs. Bramson, she said? And Miss Tolliver?

MRS. BRAMSON. That's correct. I am Mrs. Bramson. Mrs. Wadsworth Bramson the Third. This is Miss Tolliver.

MRS. GARRITY. And I am Maribeth Garrity. Ridiculous name, isn't it? All the times I've been married and I have to end up as Garrity!

MRS. BRAMSON (*disapproval*). You have been married before?

MRS. GARRITY. Oh, bless your heart, yes! I was even a princess for a while! Funny to think of now, isn't it? Such a handsome man, he was—but in those days I found it very hard to settle down. I divorced three of them before Charlie Garrity came along—a great tall man who liked to laugh. God rest his soul!

MISS TOLLIVER (*delicately*). He—has passed on?

MRS. GARRITY (*almost cheerfully*). Slapped his motorcycle right into a tree! Past eighty years old, and he had to try riding a motorcycle! Ah well—he enjoyed every second of his life, and the**re** are worse ways to go. (*Smiles.*) Dear Charlie! (*She brushes her napkin across her eyes.*)

MRS. BRAMSON. A motorcycle!?

MRS. GARRITY. He always wanted one, he said. He liked that tremendous noise they make. Well—he tried it.

MISS TOLLIVER. How awful for you!

MRS. GARRITY. Nothing about Charlie was awful, Miss Tolliver. You just had to take him as he was—and he was a wonderful man!

MISS TOLLIVER. I guess that's what we have to do with everyone—just take them as they are.

MRS. BRAMSON (*crisply*). Not necessarily. One need not take them at all if one prefers not to.

MRS. GARRITY. Ah, but that would lead to a pretty lonely life, wouldn't it? Dull, too. I can't stand for things to be dull!

(MRS. HODGES *enters carrying a tray with three glasses of fruit cocktail.*)

MRS. HODGES (*as she sets the glasses at each place*). There you are. The orange in it is fresh.

MRS. GARRITY. Oh, I do like a meal that *starts* with something!

(MRS. HODGES *takes a low candle from her tray and places it in the center of the table.*)

MRS. HODGES. It's such a gloomy day out, I thought

perhaps you'd like a candle. It always dresses up a table, doesn't it? (*She lights the candle with a match, takes her tray.*) Enjoy your fruit cocktail. I'll be back in a few minutes. (*Leaves.*)

MRS. GARRITY (*her eyes shining*). Oh, how nice to have a candle! Candles always make things *special!*

MRS. BRAMSON (*with faint approval*). I always use them on a dinner table. (*Stops, then adds more softly.*) *Used* them, I mean.

MRS. GARRITY. Candles always make me think of champagne and flowers. They sort of all go together, don't they? (*Giggles.*) I don't suppose there'll be any champagne with lunch here, though. Just as well, maybe. It always makes me hiccup. Always has. Goodness, the glasses and glasses of champagne I've had! And the hiccups! And sometimes the men would smash their glasses on the hearth after a toast to me—

MRS. BRAMSON. Indeed? A rather dramatic gesture, surely?

MRS. GARRITY (*with satisfaction*). But lovely! Men used to know how to treat an actress—I don't think they do anymore.

MISS TOLLIVER (*wide-eyed*). An actress? You were an actress, Mrs. Garrity?

MRS. GARRITY. Lord love you! Didn't you know? Maribeth Duncan, I was. New York—London—Paris—oh, I've played everywhere!

MRS. BRAMSON (*stiffly*). I believe I've heard the name.

MRS. GARRITY (*frankly*). Be a very funny thing if you hadn't. Probably saw me at one time or another. Oh, the shows I was in! Full of music and fun—not many shows like that anymore. Now everything is about people searching for their identity, whatever *that* means! Well, I've always known who I was.

MISS TOLLIVER (*shyly*). I used to read about you. In magazines, you know—and newspapers—

MRS. GARRITY. Oh, I have fat scrapbooks *full* of those clippings! Dozens and dozens of them! I'll show them to you if you like. (*Takes a bite.*) The fresh orange does make a difference, doesn't it?

MRS. BRAMSON. I don't recall ever having spoken with —an actress before.

MRS. GARRITY (*good-humoredly*). You were probably brought up to think the stage was sinful. I was, too, but it didn't make any difference. It was where I belonged. Oh, what a life that was! (*She reaches out and touches the candle gently.*) Who'd have thought that Maribeth Duncan would end up in an old folks' home!

MISS TOLLIVER (*involuntarily*). Oh, surely not! I think of it as a *retirement* home!

MRS. GARRITY (*amiably*). There's not much difference.

MRS. BRAMSON. I consider this as a *leisure* home! A place to rid oneself of all the responsibilities of running a large house, entertaining formally and frequently, supervising a staff of servants—it is a great relief to be excused from such things.

MISS TOLLIVER (*politely*). I expect it is.

MRS. BRAMSON (*her eyes on the candle*). There were great branched candelabra on *my* table—silver, they were —and always fresh flowers from our greenhouse. I arranged the flowers myself. Mr. Bramson said no one but the hostess should do the flowers. (*Her voice softens as she remembers.*) There were twelve candles altogether. White ones. Mr. Bramson would never have anything but white ones. Sometimes I thought colored ones would be pretty, but Mr. Bramson thought they looked a little cheap.

MISS TOLLIVER (*remembering*). I like colored candles. We never had any colored candles.

MRS. GARRITY. Did you use to have them on your table, too, Miss Tolliver?

MISS TOLLIVER (*quietly*). We had them everywhere, Mrs. Garrity. But they weren't for decoration, they were for light. We were poor.

MRS. BRAMSON. Oh?

MISS TOLLIVER. I remember the first house I saw that had electricity everywhere. I could hardly believe it.

MRS. GARRITY (*interested*). Where was that?

MISS TOLLIVER (*calmly*). It was when I went into service when I was thirteen. (*Looks at* MRS. BRAMSON *and speaks clearly.*) Domestic service, Mrs. Bramson. I started as a housemaid's helper.

MRS. BRAMSON (*a little unsure of herself*). Really!

MISS TOLLIVER. Yes. Really. So you see I do know something about "good servants."

MRS. BRAMSON (*a half-apology*). I had no idea when I spoke—

MISS TOLLIVER. It doesn't matter.

MRS. GARRITY (*gaily*). I bet *you* heard plenty of gossip—they always say that housemaids know everything that's going on.

MRS. BRAMSON. If one conducts oneself properly there is no gossip.

MRS. GARRITY. Ah, but who wants to do that? I like a little fun in my life! And it's the fun that makes the gossip!

MRS. BRAMSON. There are different sorts of "fun."

MRS. GARRITY. True. And I've tried them all, love. Every kind there is! (*Adds quickly.*) But nothing really *wrong,* you understand! I may have done more than my share of flirting, but I never did anything *wrong!* (*A quick sigh.*) And I guess even the flirting is all over with now. Charlie Garrity took care of that. There was nobody like him—ever! A giant of a man!

(MRS. HODGES *enters with tray holding three filled plates.*)

MRS. HODGES. All through? I'm not rushing you, am I?

MISS TOLLIVER. Not at all. Here, let me. (*She hands her fruit cup glass to* MRS. HODGES, *and takes her filled plate.* MRS. BRAMSON *and* MRS. GARRITY *sit back and allow* MRS. HODGES *to serve them.*)

MRS. HODGES. I never like to rush anyone who is eating. Meals should be a pleasure, not a gulp-and-run affair.

MRS. BRAMSON. I agree. So bad for the digestion to eat quickly.

MRS. HODGES. The candle is not bothering your eyes?

MRS. GARRITY. Oh, no!

MRS. HODGES. We don't always have them, you know. I just thought it might make lunch a little cheerier on such a gray day.

MRS. GARRITY. It's funny, the different things that candle is making us think of, Mrs. Hodges.

MRS. HODGES. Pleasant things, I hope?

MRS. GARRITY (*with a quick glance at* MISS TOLLIVER). Well—

MISS TOLLIVER (*firmly*). Yes. very pleasant.

MRS. HODGES. I'm glad. Now—do you have everything you need? There's salt there—

MISS TOLLIVER. Thank you.

(MRS. HODGES *exits, taking the tray.*)

MRS. BRAMSON (*taking a small taste*). Creamed chicken. Unimaginative.

MRS. GARRITY (*who has also taken a bite*). I think there's a touch of white wine in the sauce! Imagine! Who would expect to get white wine sauce in an old folks' home!

MRS. BRAMSON. I do wish you wouldn't insist on referring to this place as an old folks' home, Mrs. Garrity.

MRS. GARRITY. Sorry. But whatever you call it, Mrs. Bramson, that's exactly what it is. *I* think it sounds rather cozy!

MISS TOLLIVER. "Home" is a pleasant word.

MRS. GARRITY. Isn't it! You know, I never thought about it before, but the only *real* home I ever had was when I was married to Charlie! For so many years I was always traveling around someplace and living in hotels or rented apartments—oh, they were luxurious enough, but not what you'd call "homey." And that dreadful little palace of Nikki's—he was the Prince—all full of drafts and the gold bits crumbling off— Yes, there *is* a touch of wine in this!

MRS. BRAMSON. At the prices they charge they can afford it. Although I suspect it's only cooking wine.

MRS. GARRITY. It is a little expensive here, isn't it? But I don't care! Charlie did his best by me, and I still have a few good pieces of jewelry if I get stuck. That was one nice thing about being an actress years ago—the presents! I do love presents!

MRS. BRAMSON (*rather shocked*). You would *sell* your jewelry?

MRS. GARRITY. What else is it good for now? A fine sight I'd be decked out in the tiara Nikki gave me, wouldn't I? (*Giggles.*) I always called it my tiara-boom-de-aye. It made Nikki wild!

MISS TOLLIVER. But wouldn't you want to leave things like—like jewelry to your children? Or grandchildren?

Mrs. Garrity. Bless your heart, love, nothing I'd like better if I had any. Four husbands and nary a chick! There just never seemed to be time for them. After Charlie and I were married—well, it was a little late for children by then. They say you never know what you've missed, but sometimes I wonder how it would have been— And you, Mrs. Bramson. You have a family?

Mrs. Bramson (*with reserve*). I have a daughter.

Mrs. Garrity. How nice! Does she live around here? Do you see her often?

Mrs. Bramson. I really have no idea where she lives.

Mrs. Garrity (*a surprised look*). Oh.

Mrs. Bramson. She married most unsuitably—ran away, of course, since her father would never have permitted it. (*Adds quickly.*) Nor I, naturally.

Mrs. Garrity (*distressed*). And you've never heard from her?

Mrs. Bramson. She wrote once or twice right after she left. Mr. Bramson did not want me to answer the letters. Then there was a Christmas card or two—then nothing.

Mrs. Garrity (*quietly*). I see. (*Gazing at the candle again.*) But you had her for a while—as a little girl, you had her. Birthday parties, and pink frosting on the cake, and pink candles—you had all that.

Mrs. Bramson. Yes, I had all that. (*For the first time she comes close to a smile.*) She was such a pretty little girl. Her hair was almost red, and it curled. Jennifer, her name was. I called her Jenny.

Miss Tolliver (*hesitantly*). Is there no way you could find out where she is?

Mrs. Bramson (*firmly again*). Why should I do that? She cut herself off from us years ago.

Miss Tolliver. But you said she wrote—

Mrs. Bramson. Well—yes.

Miss Tolliver. And you said there were Christmas cards—

Mrs. Bramson. A few. Mr. Bramson tore them up— except one. I kept one and hid it. He never knew. There was a picture of her little boy in it. My (*her voice nearly fades*) my—grandson. (*Quickly she opens her bag and takes out a handkerchief, blowing her nose. The other two women are silent.*) I do hope I'm not catching a cold. I thought I felt a draft a while ago.

MRS. GARRITY. He would be grown now, I suppose—your grandson.

MRS. BRAMSON. No doubt.

MRS. GARRITY. With children of his own, perhaps. Your great-grandchildren! How wonderful to have great-grand-children!

(MRS. HODGES *enters with her tray.*)

MRS. HODGES. Well, ladies! How are you getting on? Ready for dessert?

MRS. BRAMSON (*in control again*). Quite ready. (*This takes effort.*) This is really very tasty, Mrs. Hodges.

MRS. HODGES. Good! I'm glad you are enjoying it. We rather pride ourselves on the food here. Will you have coffee with your dessert?

MRS. GARRITY. Could I have tea? I do like a good cup of tea! With *milk* in it!

MRS. HODGES. Of course. Mrs. Bramson?

MRS. BRAMSON. Coffee, please. Just a demitasse.

MRS. HODGES. And you, Miss Tolliver?

MISS TOLLIVER. I'll have tea, like Mrs. Garrity. Strong!

MRS. HODGES. I'll bring it right away. (MRS. HODGES *exits.*)

MRS. GARRITY. I expect you've served a lot of meals, Miss Tolliver. You said you were a housemaid, didn't you?

MISS TOLLIVER. For a while. Then for many years I was a nursemaid to the children—a nannie, really. (*She smiles.*) To the children in the house, and then to *their* children, and at the very last—even to *their* children! What dears they all are!

MRS. GARRITY. And you love them.

MISS TOLLIVER. A great deal.

MRS. GARRITY. Are they—oh, dear, perhaps I shouldn't ask! But I do so like to *know* about people! Are they pay-ing for you to stay here?

MISS TOLLIVER (*matter-of-factly*). Oh, there was no need for that. After my parents died there was no one to spend my money on except myself, and it just seemed to keep mounting up. Then I—well, to tell the truth, I made a few excellent investments. One can't help overhearing about such things in a wealthy family, you know.

MRS. GARRITY (*with delight*). You're rich!

MISS TOLLIVER (*smiling*). At least I have no financial worries.

MRS. GARRITY (*with real pleasure*). How very nice for you! Well, I always have a few good diamonds to fall back on. I knew they'd come in useful one day.

MRS. BRAMSON. But I understood you to say that Mr. Garrity left you well provided for.

MRS. GARRITY. I said Charlie did his best by me. His best wasn't too good, Mrs. Bramson. Charlie liked to spend his money as fast as he got it. Things like the motorcycle. But I'm not going to worry. I never have, and I'm not about to start now. I'll be all right.

MISS TOLLIVER (*warmly*). I'm sure you will.

(MRS. HODGES *returns with dessert and beverages on tray.*)

MRS. HODGES. Well! You three should be old friends by now! (*As she removes the plates and sets the dessert and cups around.*) Perhaps you'd like to play some cards in the lounge this afternoon—or there may be something good on television.

MRS. GARRITY. I'm not much at cards myself—and I still have to put the rest of my things away.

MISS TOLLIVER (*shyly, but she's getting braver*). You said I might see some of your scrapbooks, Mrs. Garrity.

MRS. GARRITY. Would you really like to? Oh, I'd love to show them to you! Come up to my room after lunch!

MISS TOLLIVER. I'd like that.

MRS. HODGES. And what about you, Mrs. Bramson? What will you do with yourself this afternoon?

MRS. BRAMSON. Oh—I don't really know. I have a book—

MRS. HODGES. Well, I think you'll find the lounge very comfortable, and there are excellent lights for reading.

MRS. BRAMSON. Thank you.

MRS. HODGES. Then you'll all be all right, won't you?

MRS. GARRITY. Don't you worry about us, love. We'll be fine.

Mrs. Hodges. Good! Until this evening, then. (Mrs. Hodges *takes tray and goes, leaving them with dessert.*)

Mrs. Garrity. It must be a trial for her, keeping a lot of old folks happy.

Miss Tolliver. It takes patience, I expect.

Mrs. Bramson (*rather surprised*). I suppose it does. I never thought of it quite that way before.

Mrs. Garrity. You know, I think I'm going to be very happy here! I have all my precious bits and pieces around me, and already I have two friends—

Mrs. Bramson. Did you think you might *not* like it?

Mrs. Garrity (*with a wry expression*). You must admit it's something of a comedown for a glamorous actress —and yes, I *was* glamorous, though you'd never think it now—for a glamorous actress to wind up in an old folks' home! But there didn't seem any other way. I'm not quite as spry as I was, and I do hate living alone! But I truly think I'm going to be very happy here!

Miss Tolliver. I was a little worried, too. Well, *very* worried, really. I didn't see how I could manage with no one to look out for—nothing to do all day—but, you know, I think it's going to be wonderful to be *looked* out for! To do the things *I* want to do, to sleep right through the night without listening for a child to waken and cry—oh, it does seem like such luxury!

Mrs. Garrity. What about you, Mrs. Bramson? Didn't you have any qualms about coming into—what did you call it? A leisure home?

Mrs. Bramson. Yes, that's what I called it, but perhaps it was only to make myself feel better about it.

Mrs. Garrity. There's no harm in that.

Mrs. Bramson. I've always had someone who told me what to do. Rather like Miss Tolliver, I suppose. First my parents, and then my husband. I'm not sure I could get through a day all by myself. I thought about hiring a companion—

Mrs. Garrity (*with a firm nod*). Well, you're much better off here! There'll be people to talk to, and things going on— (*Gentle teasing.*) Why, you may even decide actresses aren't such sinful creatures after all! (*Giggles.*) At least not when they get to be my age!

Miss Tolliver. What a mixed-up group we are! A

nursemaid, a famous actress, and a—a—I don't know quite how to describe you, Mrs. Bramson.

MRS. BRAMSON. At the moment I should describe myself as an old woman who suddenly feels much younger—and a little excited about starting a new life! (*Surprised.*) You know, I haven't been excited about anything in years!

MRS. GARRITY. Oh, love—every day is exciting, if you'll just relax and let it be! (*Wipes her lips with her napkin and gives a satisfied sigh.*) Well, if that's a sample of the kind of food we'll get, I shall probably gain pounds and pounds! How *wonderful* not to care about my figure anymore! Nikki—he was the prince, you know—Nikki used to span my waist with his hands. (*She smooths the front of her dress, remembering, then laughs.*) Well, he'd have trouble now! (*Places her napkin on the table.*) Shall we go?

MISS TOLLIVER. You're sure you don't mind my coming along to your room, Mrs. Garrity? I should so love to see those scrapbooks.—Imagine knowing Maribeth Duncan!

MRS. GARRITY. I wish you'd *call* me Maribeth. Mrs. Garrity is such a silly name!

MISS TOLLIVER. Thank you.

MRS. GARRITY. You must have a first name, too.

MISS TOLLIVER. I do, but it's dreadful. My name is Bernice, and I hate it! All the children have always called me Tolly.

MRS. GARRITY. Tolly, then! And you, Mrs. Bramson? But perhaps you're not a first-name person. I don't mean to be pushy—

MRS. BRAMSON. I—I wouldn't mind. My name is Olivia.

MRS. GARRITY. How pretty! Then—here we are! Maribeth, Tolly and Olivia—and I think we're going to do very well together!

(MRS. HODGES *enters, carrying a box of flowers.*)

MRS. HODGES. Miss Tolliver? This was just delivered for you.

MISS TOLLIVER (*in amazement*). For me? Oh, there must be some mistake, Mrs. Hodges. Who would send me flowers?

MRS. HODGES. It is quite clearly addressed—I'm sure it's not a mistake. There's the card.

MISS TOLLIVER. But I can't imagine who—

MRS. HODGES. Well, just open it and see. (*She exits.*)

MRS. GARRITY. Oh, there is *nothing* so exciting as getting flowers! Flowers—and champagne—and candles—

MISS TOLLIVER (*takes card from envelope and reads it aloud slowly*). "Now it's your turn to be looked out for, Tolly. Put your feet up and enjoy life! We'll come to see you soon." (*She coughs suddenly with emotion.*) It's signed by Miss Barbara, but it's really from all my children.

MRS. GARRITY (*brushing a tear of shared joy from her eyes*). Oh, how kind of them to do that, Tolly! Doesn't it make you proud?

MISS TOLLIVER (*glowing*). Very proud, Maribeth. Very proud, indeed!

MRS. BRAMSON. They must love you very much.

MISS TOLLIVER. I think they do. (*Smooths the card with her fingers, all her joy showing quietly.*) Well! I'll stop by my room and put these in water, Maribeth, and then I'll be along to see those scrapbooks. (*Pauses.*) I wonder—I have quite a few pictures of all my children—but perhaps you wouldn't want—

MRS. GARRITY. Oh, bring them! And you'll tell me about each one!

MISS TOLLIVER (*a little laugh*). That would take a long time, I'm afraid.

MRS. GARRITY. Time, Tolly dear, is something we're going to have plenty of! I'm in room twenty-eight, and I've put my name on the door. (*Pause.*) You'd be very welcome to come too, Olivia—if you care to, that is—

MRS. BRAMSON (*putting her napkin aside neatly*). I—I don't think so. Not just now, anyway. I rather thought I'd— (*She stops, and then says quickly.*) You see, I've been thinking. My lawyer will have my daughter's address. He has always had it. Mr. Bramson wanted her to *know* that he was leaving her nothing in his will. He gave instructions to the lawyer—

MRS. GARRITY (*wide-eyed*). How dreadful!

MRS. BRAMSON (*thoughtfully*). Yes, it was, wasn't it? But Mr. Bramson was a very hard man. He felt that if I had raised Jenny properly she would never have been attracted to the young man she married. My husband felt I was not a good mother.

Miss Tolliver (*quietly*). And what do *you* feel?

Mrs. Bramson (*the frozen reserve is melting fast*). I wanted Jenny to be a warm, loving person. Not like her father. She was, too! *I* never thought the marriage was so unsuitable—they were very young, and the boy hadn't much money—but we could have helped them! I wanted so *much* to help them! But there was nothing I could do— Mr. Bramson controlled all the money—I couldn't even go to see her! I never knew where she was! (*Quickly she takes a sip of water.*)

Mrs. Garrity (*placing her hand on* Mrs. Bramson's *arm*). There, there, love! It's all over and done with now. You mustn't fret over it.

Mrs. Bramson (*rises with sudden determination*). I'm not going to! I'm going to *do* something about it!

Mrs. Garrity. Bully for you!

Mrs. Bramson. I'm going to call my lawyer and get an address—and then I'm going to write. I won't blame her if she never answers—

Miss Tolliver. But I think she will.

Mrs. Garrity (*rising*). And then there's your grandson, Olivia—and perhaps his children—

Mrs. Bramson (*a happy but alarming thought*). Good heavens! If I have great-grandchildren—what shall I do? I wouldn't know how to talk to them!

Miss Tolliver (*rising, holding her flower box closely*). I would, Olivia. I would. (*Pats* Mrs. Bramson's *arm.*) Don't worry.

(Mrs. Hodges *enters with her tray.*)

Mrs. Hodges. Is there anything else I can get for you? More tea or coffee?

Mrs. Bramson. No, thank you, Mrs. Hodges. That was a delicious luncheon! You have made our first day here very happy!

Mrs. Hodges. I'm so glad!

Mrs. Garrity. And the candle, Mrs. Hodges! Oh, we did enjoy the candle!

Mrs. Hodges (*pleased*). I thought you might. There's something about a candle on the table—

Miss Tolliver. Thank you for bringing my flowers in.
And we'll see you later on.

Mrs. Hodges. Yes. Later on.

(The three women leave the room. Mrs. Hodges watches them go, smiling, then she cups the candle flame in her hand and blows it out, as the lights fade out with it.)

CURTAIN

9 780874 409840